G O D

CREATOR OF FAMILIES

Philip and Maria Steers
Grandpa and Grandma Steers

PRESS

God, Creator of Families
by Philip and Maria Steers

Printed in the United States of America

ISBN 1-594677-02-6
Library of Congress Control Number: 2004095494

www.xulonpress.com

PRAISE BE TO THE
GOD OF OUR LORD
JESUS CHRIST, THE
FATHER OF GLORY,
THE FATHER TO WHOM
ALL POWER BELONGS,
THE FATHER OF WHOM
EVERY FAMILY IN
HEAVEN AND ON EARTH
IS NAMED...

With loving prayers
Phil + Marion Steere

Ephesians 3:14-21
John 14:23

To

our precious children

Philip III
Yolan
David
Marion

and their children

Elise
Philip IV
Nathaniel
Jeffrey
Jason
Jennifer
Jonathan
James
Christalyn
Benjamin
Solomon
Corrie
Steven
Emily
Nathan

and to all their precious children
Baby Seven Yolan and others to come

Acknowledgments

*T*hanks be to God for His wonderful teaching on how He planned us to live in happy and united families. Heartfelt thanks are due to our church, Grace Fellowship Church in Snellville, GA, whose call to us for action comes from Psalm 78:4-6:

> *"Telling to the generation to come the praises of the Lord, and His strength and His wonderful works that He has done.*
> *For . . . He commanded our fathers, that they should make them known to their children:*
> *That the generation to come might know them,*
> *The children who would be born,*
> *That they may arise and declare them to their children . . .*

At our advanced age we dedicate ourselves to this task for the love of our children and grandchildren and great-grandchildren and all the following generations. In our day, when many of our national leaders ignore how God has planned the family there is an urgency to point out — from the beginning — the teachings of His written Word.[1]

Heartfelt thanks goes to our children, together with their spouses, who — in their true loving concern for our family — have always sincerely indicated their expectations concerning the example that our lives should be to them. This is how they have inspired us again and again to go to our knees to study God's Word and to pray the prayer that has become our family prayer:

"Search me, O God, and know my heart:
Try me, and know my anxieties,
And see if there is any wicked way in me,
And lead me in the way everlasting." Psalm 139:23, 24

Members of the families of our four children and teachers at our church and friends have reviewed the manuscript of this book. Unusual and powerful help came from our dear widowed neighbor lady who does not agree with what was written. In her kindness she studied through it in detail. She helped us to see how the book should speak to those, also, who are of a different persuasion. Furthermore, she gave us great insights into making the message complete by keeping it in the fore-front in the introduction, in the body of the book and in the conclusion.

Heartfelt thanks are due to our son, Philip III, who studied the manuscript and gave us excellent insights and coached us all along with his expertise in the computer. Then, our grandson Nate, Senior at The Citadel, during his few free days from school, did valuable work of review, especially in clarifying complicated sentences.

Table of Contents

Preface

*A*ll mankind shares a deep longing for a happy home where their family enjoys living in loving unity. This book studies God's plan for the family. It starts from the beginning of the Bible and continues throughout its history. God loves the family, He takes care of it and He safely guides it toward its future life in His heavenly home.

The message of this book is crucial for our nation. At this time in America unhappy people want to change the structure of the family. They ignore that from the beginning of the creation of mankind, in every nation, in every culture, in every religion all over the world marriage was celebrated as a man and a woman becoming "one flesh." In America until now marriage was always celebrated as "one man with one woman united for life," by couples looking forward to the miracle of having their own children. Changing God's plan leads to the break up of unity with much sadness and disappointment.

. Since about the 1960-s godless citizens have been working hard to take God and His laws out of public knowledge. More than 150 ago Senator Daniel Webster predicted what now has become reality in America:

> *If truth is not diffused, error will be.*
> *If God and His Word are not known and received, the devil and his works will gain ascendancy . . .*
> *If the evangelical volume does not reach every hamlet, the pages of a corrupt and licentious literature will.*
> *If the power of the Gospel does not impact the breadth and length of this land, anarchy and misrule,*

degradation and misery, corruption and darkness will reign without mitigation or end. [Fuess, D.W., 289-290. Summary of the Plymouth oration. 1823]

Urgently, we need to return to the truth of God's Word to clear up the present confusion concerning how to establish happy, united families in our nation. The family is the foundation of any nation.

In this book we, as grandparents, leave behind our love for our children and their children. Our heartfelt prayer for them is for the assurance that the God of the Bible is the loving heavenly Father who sent His Son to bless every family on earth. His blessing will rest on their family as they teach their children to live according to His Word. God's Son went to the cross and rose again to save us from our own sinful hearts and to make us into a loving, obedient family of children to the heavenly Father. The earthly family of the heavenly Father is *"the church of the living God."* Its members are all those who live in a heavenly relationship with the heavenly Father through His beloved Son, Jesus Christ.

> *"Therefore let that abide in you which you heard from the beginning. If what you heard from the beginning abides in you, you also will abide in the Son and in the Father."* 1 John 2:24
>
> *"And whatever we ask we receive from Him, because we keep His commandments and do those things that are pleasing in His sight.*
>
> *And this is His commandment that we should believe on the name of His Son Jesus Christ and love one another, as He gave us commandment."* 1 John 3:22, 23

With loving prayers

Philip and Maria Steers
Grandpa and Grandma Steers

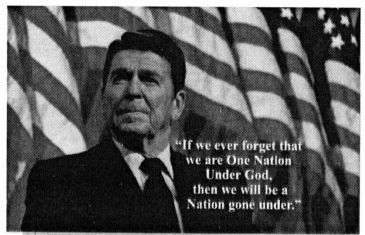

"If we ever forget that we are One Nation Under God, then we will be a Nation gone under."

The family has always been the cornerstone of American society.

Our families nurture, preserve and pass on to each succeeding generation the values we share and cherish, values that are the foundation for our freedoms. In the family, we learn our first lessons of God and man, love and discipline, rights and responsibilities, human dignity and human frailty.

Our families give us daily examples of these lessons being put into practice. In raising and instructing our children, in providing personal and compassionate care for the elderly, in maintaining the spiritual strength of religious commitment among our people—in these and other ways, America's families make immeasurable contributions to America's well-being.

Today more than ever, it is essential that these contributions not be taken for granted and that each of us remember that the strength of our families is vital to the strength of our nation.

Ronald Reagan

The Rebirth of America, published by
The Arthur S. DeMoss Foundation, 1986, page 97

THE GOD OF THE BIBLE

PROMISES VICTORY TO

THE FAMILY

while His enemy works to destroy it

Philip and Maria Steers
Grandpa and Grandma Steers

God promises victory to the family

*T*he God of the Bible, the heavenly Father, leads His family to victory, while His enemy works to destroy it. He sent His beloved Son to bless every family on earth.

"Jesus said: 'I have come that they may have life and that they may have it more abundantly." John 10:10b

"Therefore choose life, that both you and your children may live." " Deuteronomy 30:19

America stands at the crossroads.

God has given us the freedom of choice. God has given us the freedom to choose life, but today in our society many are choosing to reject God and the life that He offers. The founding fathers of America have established our constitutional republic on the principles laid down in the Bible, God's Word. Our citizens were honored or punished according to these principles until the 1960-s. Then it became obvious that godless citizens were working to erase all memory of our great Judeo-Christian heritage out of public knowledge, out of our public life and out of our schools. There has never been such an open rebellion against the God of the Bible and His laws in all of America's history.

It is becoming more and more obvious, that our nation is made up of two opposing groups of people, those who choose life and those who choose death. The apostle John's words are most timely:

> *"We know that we belong to God and that the whole world is under the rule of the Evil One.*
> *We know that the Son of God has come and has given us understanding so that we know the true God. Our lives are in the true God and in His Son Jesus Christ. This is the true God and this is eternal life."*
> 1 John 5:19, 20 TEV

America is experiencing the truth of Jesus' words about "the rule of the Evil One." He called him "the thief" whose purpose is to steal, kill and destroy.[2] Under the rule

of the "Evil One" false apostles make themselves look like true apostles of Christ. Even Satan is able to change himself to look like an angel of light.."[3] "The thief" is out to rob God of His glory. He blinds people into thinking that they can be good without God. But goodness belongs to God alone, no one is able to reproduce it apart from Him.

"The thief" is working to destroy the family the way God planned it to be as "one man with one woman united for life." He robs married couples from faithful commitment to each other. They think that "good" will result if they divorce. "The thief" seduces boys and girls, men and women into immoral life styles outside of marriage, cutting them off from God's blessing. The babies out of such unions are either destroyed or come into the world as so called "unwanted children." Most of them are raised by single mothers because the father does not accept his responsibility for them. "The thief" fools people into rejecting the reality that our Creator formed our human body to be male and female. He lures these blinded people into same-gender "marriages" or "unions" robbing them of the approval of God. They give themselves over to sexual lust rather than to the privilege of bringing to life children to the pleasure of God.

In America there is much confusion concerning what happy family life should be. Families are falling apart because members insist on having their own way instead of looking out for the common good of their family. When family members no longer look out for the good of their own, they no longer are able to self-lessly look out for the good of our nation. America's strength can return only as we return to the great God of the Bible, on whose wisdom and love this nation was founded. Only as we stand united "under God" can we continue to be a strong, united America to withstand the attacks of those who come against us.

Good news for fathers and mothers

God has good news for the fathers and mothers of families "who live in the true God." In The Ten Commandments "written with the finger of God" [4] He promised His mercy to the children of those fore-fathers who love Him and obey His commandments.[5] America to this day enjoys God's mercies because of the obedience of the founding fathers, who established our laws on God's laws written in the Bible, in order to invoke God's favor on our nation. The three branches of America's government are based on Isaiah 33:22

> *"For the Lord is our Judge,*
> *The Lord is our Lawgiver,*
> *The Lord is our King;*
> *He will save us."*

This is the God whose wisdom our founding fathers were seeking when they formed the judicial, legislative and executive branches of America's government. They knew that one man alone is not capable of governing the nation in the right way. They were convinced that by seeking God's wisdom together in His written Word He would lead them to the right decisions. As a result they founded the longest ongoing constitutional republic in the history of the world.

In 1892 the United States Supreme Court concluded after ten years of research covering America's historical founding documents:

> *"Our laws and our institutions must necessarily be based upon and embody the teachings of the Redeemer of mankind. It is impossible that it should be otherwise! And in this sense and to this extent our institutions are emphatically Christian."* [The Trinity Decision]

God made America the greatest nation on earth because its citizens were taught to obey God according to His written Word.[6]

God offers His same kindness and blessing to every nation and every family and every individual. There is not even one of us who deserves God's blessings because we all have failed to obey God's commandments and have fallen short of the perfect obedience that He requires of us in His written Word, the Bible.[7] But in His kindness toward us, on His cross God's beloved Son took all that we have done wrong on Himself. Then from His risen glory He poured out on us His Holy Spirit, who enables us to live according to God's written Word.

As we learn to enjoy God's love and forgiveness, our hearts overflow with love and forgiveness toward others around us. This is how the Lord Jesus is able to save families that are falling apart. He enables us to humble ourselves in forgiving one another and doing helpful deeds of service even to those who have hurt our feelings or were rude to us.[8] The Lord Jesus who has assured us of God's forgiveness in our own heart is able to do the same miracle in other hearts as we love them and pray for them. Our God is "the God who hears and answers our prayers.[9]

To the Steers family God's promise of His mercies is especially precious because in 1998 we were devastated by the tragic death of David, our second son.[10] However, — in our sorrow — to our surprise he was the one who provided for us the most powerful comfort. Through his unique notations in his well-studied Bible he left behind the treasure of his intimate knowledge of God. He left us with a challenge that keeps healing our hearts, broken at his death. We now have a pressing desire to know "the God of the Bible" not only as the heavenly Father of each one of us individually, but also to know Him as the Father of our whole family. He sent His Son Jesus to bless our family and every family on earth, whether in joy or in sorrow.

God also showed us His mercy in that shortly before his death David wrote us a letter, not knowing that they will be his last words to us. From his loving heart as father he told us of the special promises God had given him concerning his children. He wanted to express his faith in these promises publicly. David wrote these words with deep conviction based on Joshua 24:15c: "As for me and my house [my family] we will be baptized and serve the Lord." His heart was fixed on God for "family obedience," his and Leann's earnest prayer that their children would listen to their teaching and be united in their hearts with them to live in a way that brings pleasure to God.

"Family obedience," united family, is the prayer of all the parents who believe in God's beloved Son, born of a virgin, crucified for our sin and risen to glory to be the Lord and Savior of the whole world.[11] Every lawfully married, faithful couple, "one man with one woman united for life," — whether they have children or not — is a picture of God's love for His Church. It is made up of God's people who gather together with united hearts, **"with one accord in one place,"** [12] to worship the God of the Bible. The Church is the Bride of Christ, the Bridegroom is the Lord Jesus Christ in love with His Bride, His Church:

> *"Christ* **[the Son of God]** *loved the church and gave Himself for her."* Ephesians 5:25

Biblical marriage is a holy relationship because it is the earthly picture of the Church's heavenly relationship with God's beloved Son. The Bible begins with a marriage and ends with a marriage. The first marriage was between the first man and the first woman, Adam and Eve.[13] The last marriage will take place in heaven at the joy-filled wedding feast of the Lamb and the true Church.[14]

Jesus did His first miracle at the marriage feast in Cana of Galilee.[15] There, Jesus began to reveal His glory to His disciples. The wine ran out to the embarrassment of the host of the wedding party. Jesus changed water into wine, better than that which was served before. He wanted the guests to continue their joyful celebration of the bride and the groom. God is present at every wedding.

At weddings family and friends gather together to acknowledge God's blessing on the man and the woman who are uniting their hearts and lives to establish a family to His glory. All over the world those who believe *"that Jesus is the Christ, the Son of God."* [16] gather together to unite themselves as the international family of the heavenly Father, "the church of the living God," *"the pillar and foundation of the truth."* [17] Our Lord Jesus is working in our hearts — as He calls us out of this sinful world — to recreate us into His likeness. The best wine that He provides for us is His precious blood shed for our sin. Together, in our congregations, we get to know Him more and more fully from His Word. He enables us through His Holy Spirit to become obedient to the heavenly Father like He was, when He went to the cross for us.

God created father-mother families

From the beginning God created the man and the woman for His eternal purpose, for Him to have a family of children who love Him and live for His pleasure. For same-gender unions it is impossible to bring children into the world for God's pleasure. The Bible tells us how God created the man and the woman in His own likeness:

> *So God created man in His own image; in the image*
> *of God He created him: male and female He created them.*
> *And God blessed them, and God said to them, 'Be*
> *fruitful and multiply, fill the earth . . .*
> *Then God saw everything that He had made, and*
> *indeed it was very good."* Genesis 1:27, 28a, 31a

Think about this command: "Be fruitful and multiply, fill the earth . . . " God created man to fill the earth by having children. For same gender unions this is not possible. Their families will die out with them.

So then, man by himself could not be complete without the woman. After creating Adam God said:

> *"It is not good that man should be alone . . ."*
> Genesis 2:18

Therefore — in His wisdom — God created Eve for Adam in a special way. God had formed Adam from the dust of the ground and breathed into his nostrils the breath of life to make him into a living being.[18] But He created Eve in such a way that she could be a well-suited companion and helper to complete him, a wife, a mother, a homemaker, to be a living part of him:

> *And the Lord caused a deep sleep to fall on Adam,*
> *and he slept; and God took one of his ribs, and closed up*
> *the flesh in its place.*
> *Then the rib which the Lord God had taken from*
> *the man He made into a woman, and He brought her to*
> *the man.*
> *And Adam said:*
> *'This is now bone of my bones and flesh of my flesh;*
> *She shall be called Woman,*
> *Because she was taken out of Man."* Genesis 2:21-23

God's Word explains to us why men and women have such a powerfully strong desire to find one special soul-mate for themselves among those of the opposite gender. It is God who has put this desire into our hearts. There are so many handsome young men and so many beautiful women, but when God causes true love to be born in our heart, only that "special one" will do. That special one is the one for whom God made us.

God designed the union of a man and a woman for the propagation and survival of mankind. Even nature teaches us the truth about the way God created the male and the female genders:

> *"A man . . . reflects the image and glory of God. But woman reflects the glory of man;*
>
> *For man was not created from woman, but woman from man.*
>
> *Nor was man created for woman's sake, but woman was created for man's sake . . .*
>
> *In our life in the Lord, however, woman is not independent of man, nor is man independent of woman.*
>
> *For as woman was made from man, in the same way man is born of woman, and all things come from God."* 1 Corinthians 11:7-12 TEV

When the Lord God Himself was on earth in the Person of the Lord Jesus Christ, He confronted us with these words:

> *"Haven't you read this scripture? 'In the beginning the Creator made them male and female,*

and said, 'For this reason a man will leave his
father and mother and unite with his wife and the two will
become one?

So then they are no longer two, but one. Man must
not separate, then, what God has joined together . . ."
Matthew 19:4-6 TEV

Notice the words: " . . . the two shall become one flesh, they are no longer two, but one flesh." (NKJ) If there is divorce, the Lord Jesus added, *"it is because of the hardness of your hearts."* [19] The words of the Lord Jesus about the married relationship are mighty words of command. This special relationship is for only two people, for that one man with that one woman, not with anyone else. It is a most intimate relationship, not for public display. It is a most special relationship in which the husband and the wife discover one another and learn to enjoy one another in a most unique, God-given way. It is a relationship that unites for life the one man and the one woman with the love that comes from God. This is that forgiving love whereby — while we were yet sinners — God's beloved Son died for us. He commands not to cut apart a man and a woman whom God Himself has joined together into "one flesh." God's approval and blessing rests only on this one biblical law: "One man with one woman united for life."

Men and women bend toward disobedience

From the beginning child-bearing was God's original intent for marriage. The "Evil One" however seduced the first man and the first woman into disobeying God by eating the fruit from "the tree of the knowledge of good and evil," instead of eating from "the tree of life." Because of their disobedience Adam and Eve were estranged from God and brought His judgment on themselves and on all mankind. And as mankind multiplied he continued to display his inclination toward disobedience.

"Then the Lord saw that the wickedness of man
was great in the earth and that every imagination of the

thoughts of his heart was only evil continually . . . and the earth was filled with violence . . . And the Lord was grieved in His heart . . ." Genesis 6:5, 6, 11

When the imagination of the thoughts of man's heart became evil, it grieved the heart of God. At present in our daily news we have plenty of evidence that in our nation there is much to grieve God's heart. Through the media, literature. Computers, TV, etc. our homes are invaded with what is being fabricated in "the imagination of the thoughts of human hearts." People fill their minds with human ideas from fiction and senseless TV shows. We are tempted to pay more attention to our own ideas and desires, rather than to applying ourselves to understand God's wisdom from His Word and from His amazing Creation made for mankind's benefit.

The Bible warns us that as people multiply on the earth they will become more and more wicked.[20] God is deeply concerned about what is going on in our hearts and even in our most secret thoughts.[21] He grieves that in the last days[22] people will turn away from listening to His truth, that *"they will **not listen to what the Bible says, but will blithely** [blindly] *follow their own misguided ideas."*[23] They do not seek God's wisdom from His written Word the way America's wise founding fathers did. God alone is able to set us free from our slavery to our bent to disobedience. Deep down inside every human being knows that God's wrath rests on disobedience to His laws. But it is easier to keep busy rather than to find out from God's written Word how to escape His wrath and how to enjoy Him and His blessings forever.

God raised up faithful fathers

In His mercy God always raised up faithful fathers who led their children to obey His Word. When God recorded His grief with mankind in Genesis chapter 6, He also preserved for us the history of one father, Noah. This exceptional father was a pleasure to God not a grief to Him. He believed God's warning of His coming judgment by a worldwide flood, even while every one else around him ignored it. He listened to God's instruction and built an ark to save his family from the flood of God's wrath.

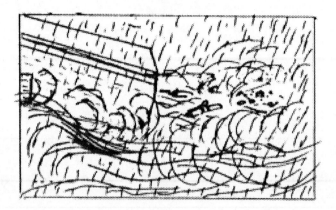

While the flood waters destroyed all the other families around him, the same waters floated Noah and his family in the ark to safety. God sent the flood to prove — in the midst of His wrath — His saving power and mercy toward a father and his family who obeyed His Word.

When our David was five years old he told us: "God sent the flood to make Noah's ark float." Yes, God makes a difference between the believer and the unbeliever. While He displays His just indignation on the disobedient, He also shows His favor toward the obedient. His mercy is to His people who obey Him. After the flood *"the Lord who had mercy on them"* put a beautiful rainbow up in the sky for them. It was His sign to Noah and his family and to all their descendants that *"with everlasting kindness He would have mercy on them . . . and that His covenant of peace would never be removed."*[24]

Abraham, the father of the biblical family

Another father stands out in Genesis chapter 12. He is Abraham, whom God chose to carry out His original intent of blessing on "the father-mother-children" family. Before Abraham had children and while his wife, Sarah, was barren God said to Abraham:

> " . . . *I will make you a great nation, I will bless you . . . and you shall be a blessing . . . and in you all the families of the earth shall be blessed . . .* " Genesis 12:2,3

> *"Do not be afraid, Abram, I am your shield and your exceeding great reward . . .*
> *One* [**Christ**] *who will come from your own body shall be your heir. Look now toward heaven and number the stars if you are able to number them . . . So shall your descendants be . . .*
> *And Abraham believed in the Lord God, and He counted it to him for righteousness."* Genesis 15:1, 4-6; Galatians 3:16

Abraham believed God's promise concerning that One from his own body, the One who would come to bless every family on earth and his faith pleased God. ***"And he was called the friend of God."***[25]

God gave Abraham a special place of honor, an intimate relationship with Him, because he became a father who trained his children to live according to God's Word:

> *"And the Lord God said, 'Shall I hide from Abraham what I am doing since Abraham shall surely become a great and mighty nation, and all the nations* [family groups] *of the earth shall be blessed in him?*
> *For I have known him, in order that he may command his children and his household after him that they keep the way of the Lord, to do righteousness and justice that the Lord may bring on Abraham what He has spoken to him.* " Genesis 18:17-19

God tested Abraham's and Sarah's faith by making them wait for a very long time for that son that He had promised them. Abraham and Sarah became old and way past the age when it would be possible for them to have a baby. But Abraham believed that God would keep His Word and give him that son, whom God Himself named ***"Isaac" "Laughter."***[26] He believed that God would bring new life out of his own body that was as good as dead and that Sarah's barrenness could not hinder God from giving them that baby boy that He had promised them.[27] The miraculous birth of Isaac taught Abraham that his God is *"the God who gives life to the dead."*[28]

When Isaac was a teenager God again tested Abraham's faith that He has the power to raise the dead. He required Abraham to bring Him a whole burnt offering, a *"holocaust"*[29] on His altar and that sacrifice was to be Isaac, *"his only begotten son, the son of his love through whom he would receive the promises."*[30] This sacrifice would allow this earthly father to understand the pain of the heavenly Father's "Father-heart," when He would — in the future — offer up His own Son, Abraham's Great Descendant as the "burnt offering" for our sin. Abraham did place his beloved Isaac on the altar and for his obedience God made Himself known to him in a new way.

God rewarded Abraham's obedience by sparing Isaac and providing a ram to be placed on the altar as a burnt offering instead of Isaac, his son. In this act of mercy God foretold to Abraham that his Great Descendant, God's own Son, would offer Himself in our place to be the perfect "burnt offering," or "holocaust," to turn away God's wrath from our sin and to provide in our place all that God requires of us.

Then God bestowed — under His own oath — this special blessing on Abraham:

"Now I know that you fear God, since you have not withheld your son, your only son from Me . . .

By Myself I have sworn, the Lord says, because you have done this and have not held back your son, your only son,

Blessing will I bless you, and multiplying I will multiply your descendants as the stars of the heaven and as the sand which is on the seashore; and your descendants shall possess the gate of their enemies.

In your Seed all the nations [family groups] *of the earth shall be blessed, because you have obeyed My voice.'*

And Abraham called the name of that place The Lord Will Provide . . ." Genesis 22:12, 14, 16-18

The promised Savior from Abraham's own body would enable his descendants "to possess the gate of their enemies," setting them free from slavery to "the thief." God's oath became very precious to the Jewish people. They passed it on from generation to generation. Hundreds of years later, when John the Baptist, the herald of the Messiah was born, his father Zacharias, praised God for keeping the oath He made to Abraham with these words:

"Blessed be the Lord God of Israel, for He visited . . . His people . . .

To perform the mercy He promised to our fathers
And to remember His holy covenant,
The oath which He swore to our father Abraham,
To grant us that we
Being delivered from the hand of our enemies,
Might serve Him without fear,
In holiness and righteousness before Him all the days of our life." Luke 1:68, 72-75

Zacharias understood that the Messiah would deliver God's

people from the power of the "Evil One," who incites rebellion against God in human hearts. The Messiah would set them free so they could serve God without fear — from the persecution of the "Evil One" — in holiness and righteousness all the days of their life. From generation to generation the Jewish people passed on the joyful news of God's oath to Abraham that their Messiah would be born as Abraham's Offspring from his own body. The promised Savior would empower God's children to withstand all temptations by being a united, loving, obedient family to the heavenly Father. Each individual family would partake of this blessing.[31]

The Lord Jesus spoke of Abraham's encounter with God and said to the Jews:

> *"Your father Abraham rejoiced to see My day and he saw it and was glad."* John 8:56

Abraham, example to all of us

Abraham's faith in God's promises is an example for all of us. He proved his faith in "the God who raises the dead" by his obedience to God's command to place his beloved Isaac on the altar ready to offer him up as a burnt offering. Because of his obedience God made Abraham the father of all those who believe His promises like he did.[32]

> *"As the Scripture says, "I have made you father of many nations." . . . Abraham believed the God who brings the dead to life . . .*
> *He was almost a hundred years old ; but his faith did not weaken when he thought of his body, which was already practically dead, or of the fact that Sarah could not have any children.*
> *His faith did not leave him, and he did not doubt God's promise; his faith filled him with power, and he gave praise to God.*
> *For he was absolutely sure that God would . . . do what He had promised.*

> *That is why Abraham, through faith, "was accepted as righteous by God."* [33]
> *The words "he was accepted as righteous" were not written for him alone.*
> *They were written also for us who are to be accepted as righteous who believe in him* [God] *who raised Jesus our Lord from death.*
> *He was given over to die because of our sins, and was raised up to life to put us right with God."* Romans 4:16-25 TEV

Abraham was able to place his beloved Isaac on the altar because he believed that his God raises the dead, that He would give Isaac's life back to him. God expresses His approval of us in our heart when we confess with our lips that the crucified, risen Son of God is our Lord.[34] God's children come to life by God's miraculous life-giving power and are preserved in life by God's miraculous saving power like Isaac was.

> *"Now we, brethren, as Isaac was, are children of the promise."* Galatians 4:28

God had promised Abraham that his children would be as the stars of heaven. Isaac was the firstborn son among them. Who are these descendants of Abraham who are as the stars of heaven?

> *"Lift up your eyes on high and see who has created these stars, who brings out their host in number, He calls them by name, by the greatness of His might and by the strength of His power not one is missing."* Isaiah 40:26

In the book of Revelation the risen Lord of glory has seven stars in His right hand which are *"the messengers of the seven churches."* These are the faithful disciples who publish the good news of the Lord Jesus Christ.[35]

The New Testament tells how we, too, become "stars" in Jesus' right hand:

". . .God is always at work in you to make you willing and able to obey His own purpose.

Do everything without complaining or arguing, that you may be innocent and pure, as God's perfect children who live in a world of crooked and perverse people.

You must shine among them like stars lighting up the dark sky, as

you offer them the message of life. If you do so, I shall have reason to rejoice in you on the Day of Christ. . .
" Philippians 2:13-16 TEV

Abraham believed God's promise concerning the One from his own body whom the Father would send to bless every family on earth. So then we — who believe like Abraham did — and publish our faith in God's message of "life from above," we are the stars whom God promised to Abraham.

" Rejoice because your names are written in heaven." Luke 10:20

This is the faith that our son David had in his heart at his unexpected death. In his last letter he left behind for us his desire that he wanted to express his faith publicly in God's promises concerning his family. He and Leann were in the midst of a very special time of preparation and thought because they were expecting their third child, Baby Solomon Isaac in about three weeks. To us, David's parents, it is especially meaningful that he and Leann chose the name "Isaac" for their expected baby son. In his letter David wrote with deep conviction that God's everlasting covenant with Abraham in Genesis 17:7 applies to his family. It was within this covenant that God promised to give to Abraham and Sarah a baby son ***"Isaac," "Laughter"*** by miracle in their old age. These are the words of the everlasting covenant that David took by faith as God's blessing on his family:

"I will establish My covenant between Me and you and your descendants after you in all their generations,

for an everlasting covenant, to be God to you and to your descendants after you."

David rejoiced in God's promise to Abraham: "I am your God and I am your children's God forever." David believed that the God of Abraham kept His promise when He sent His Son to bless every family on earth. David had the assurance that he and his family belonged to that Savior. In his letter he kept repeating: "Remember, Mom, the Holy Spirit is <u>to you and to your children. Acts 2:39</u>." He always underlined <u>"to you and to your children</u>." God fulfilled this covenant promise ***"to be God to you,"*** when He poured out His Holy Spirit on His disciples, Abraham's descendants, on the Day of Pentecost. Filled with the Holy Spirit Peter declared publicly that even though Abraham's Great Descendant, the Lord Jesus Christ was crucified, He was raised from the dead and was exalted to the right hand of the Father. From His glory He poured out His Holy Spirit in order to make Him, the crucified, risen King of the Jews known to our hearts as the Lord God Most High, the God of Abraham, the God of Isaac and the God of Jacob.[36]

Peter concluded his message with this invitation:

> *"Repent, and let every one of you be baptized in the name of Jesus Christ for the forgiveness of your sins, and you shall receive the gift of the Holy Spirit.*
> *For the promise is to you and to your children . . ."*
> Acts 2:38, 39

Our son David believed that the great God whom Peter preached is the God of his family and he wanted to express his faith publicly. He based his faith on the words of the apostle Peter, that the great God who had poured out His Holy Spirit at Pentecost is the same God who made this everlasting covenant with Abraham: "I am your God and I am your children's God, I am the God of your family forever." I believe with David that the God of Abraham, the God of the Bible — even now — still is the God of his family. And the God of the Bible is God even in times of tragedy. He is the God of each of us individually and He is the God of our whole family, also, according to His Word to Abraham.

God's children are born by miracle

All of God's children are born by miracle into His family like Isaac was born to Abraham and Sarah. Abraham believed God's promise: ***"I will bless Sarah and give you a son by her. . .***[37]And Sarah ***"judged Him faithful who had promised."*** [38]

> *"Therefore from one man* **[Abraham]***, and him as good as dead, were born as many as the stars of the sky in multitude, innumerable . . ."* Hebrews 11:12

Abraham and Sarah are our examples how to believe God for our children. At the grave of Lazarus, before He raised him from the dead, Jesus said to Martha:

> *"Did I not say unto you that if you would believe you would see the glory of God?"* John 11:40

God displays His glory in our children as we believe His promises by teaching them to our children. God works miracles in hearts at the hearing of God's Word:[39]

> *"The Word was God . . . and the world was made through Him . . . He came to His own and His own received Him not, but as many as received Him to them He gave the right to become the children of God, to those*
> *who believe on His name, who were born, not of blood, nor of the will of the flesh, nor of the will of man, but of God."* John 1:11-13

It is a miracle of God, the Father when we receive His only begotten Son into our heart and life. As we believe that His beloved Son is His Living Word to us He receives us into His own family and recreates us into a new person, as His own child.

God's children inherit Abraham's blessing

All who were "born of God" inherit the promise that God made to Abraham: "I am your God and your children's God forever."

> *"For you are all sons of God through faith in Christ Jesus. For as many of you as were baptized into Christ have put on Christ, . . . for you all are one in Christ Jesus.*
> *And if you are Christ's then you are Abraham's seed, and heirs according to God's promise."* Galatians 3:26-28

God keeps His promise to Abraham

Throughout their troublesome history God faithfully took care of Abraham's offspring to show that He faithfully cares for every family who turns to Him. The God of the Bible had made an everlasting covenant with Abraham: "I am your God and your children's God ." [40] Abraham passed on this blessing to his son Isaac. Among Isaac's two sons the older one, Esau, only cared about his immediate physical needs, not about God. But the younger one, Jacob, — more than anything in his life — set his heart on assuring God's blessing on himself and on his descendants. And so — relying on his mother's clever plan — he tricked his father, Isaac, to pass on the blessing of Abraham to him, rather than to his older brother. But God knew Jacob's earnest longing for His blessing and He met his heart-cry with this assurance:

> *" . . . I will be the God of all the families of Israel and they shall be My people . . ."* Jeremiah 31:1

"Israel" is Jacob's new name to show that he had finally fully submitted himself to God. There was much intrigue in Jacob's family life and among his twelve sons. When God called for a famine in the Promised Land, He allowed Joseph, Jacob's favorite son, to be carried away as a slave into Egypt. There He raised him up to be ruler over rich Egypt, so that he was able to provide there a safe place for his family. In Egypt the God of Jacob miraculously kept his family separate from the Egyptians, to preserve them in twelve tribes [twelve family groups] as His chosen people.

After some years a Pharaoh came to power who hated Jehovah, the God of Israel. He commanded all the Jewish baby boys to be killed, but there was a godly father and mother who believed God for their baby boy, Moses. They were not afraid of the king's command and put their faith into action to save their baby. God rewarded their faith and saved Moses by miracle.[41]

The Lord God saw the cruelty of Pharaoh toward His people in Egypt and heard their cry.[42] At the miraculously burning bush He made Himself known to Moses by the name *"The God of Abraham, the God of Isaac and the God of Jacob."*[43] This is the name whereby the Lord Jesus Christ also called the God of the Bible.[44] This is the God who raised up Moses to become the leader of His people.[45] This is the God who executed His terrible judgment against the gods of Egypt by great plagues. And this is the God who showed the fathers of His people's families through Moses how to escape His wrath. God had promised that He would make a difference between the rebellious Egyptians and His believing people.[46] He gave the fathers this command:

> *". . . every man shall take himself a lamb, according to the house of his father, a lamb for a household. . .*
>
> *Pick out and take lambs for yourselves according to your families, and kill the Passover lamb.*
>
> *And you shall take a bunch of hyssop, dip it in the blood that is in the basin, and strike the lintel and the two doorposts with the blood of the lamb that is in the basin. And none of you shall go out of the door of his house until the morning.*
>
> *Then they shall eat the flesh on that night; roasted in fire . . .*
>
> *For the Lord will pass through to strike the Egyptians, but when He sees the blood on the lintel and the two doorposts, the Lord will pass over the door and not allow the destroyer to come into your houses to strike you.*
>
> *. . . And you shall observe this ordinance for you*

and your sons forever.
. . . And it shall be, when your children say to you,
'What do you mean by this service?'
That you shall say, 'It is the Passover sacrifice of
the Lord, who passed over the houses of the children of
Israel in Egypt when He struck the Egyptians and deliv-
ered our households . . .
This is that night of the Lord, a solemn observance
for all the children of Israel throughout their generations.
Exodus 12:8,23-27, 42

God's Passover was to be kept by the father for his family, for his wife and their children. This solemn celebration was never forgotten by the Jewish people. Throughout all their numberless trials in their history — from then on to this day — they faithfully kept the Passover feast year by year. Every year they faithfully gather together as a family to remember the Passover. They are an example to us by the way they have kept powerfully united families and a miraculously surviving nation by remembering together what God has done for them in delivering them from their slavery in Egypt. And each year they fill their hearts with fresh hope that their Lord God, the God of Israel will save them out of their present sufferings and bring them to that perfect city, the New Jerusalem, that He had promised to build for them and for all mankind.[47]

In America we have our Day of Thanksgiving when with our families we gather together to celebrate our great Judeo-Christian history. The Pilgrims in England were not allowed to obey the Word of God according to the dictate of their conscience. For this reason they bravely risked their lives to cross the great ocean. They came to America to establish a nation with the liberty of worshiping the God of the Bible and to live according to His laws written in His Word. America's fore-fathers are an example to us with their heroic faith in God and with their accomplishments by their united prayers and their faith in Him. Their first concern was to establish schools where the children were taught the Bible. Our families here in America have a great history to celebrate of God's mighty acts for our nation. We have good reason to teach our children to trust and honor God by obeying Him. It is the God of the Bible who made America the present leading nation on earth.

Of late, however, the people of the "Evil One" have successfully taken America's rich Judeo-Christian history out of the text books of our schools. They are working hard to rob our nation of the knowledge of God and His commandments. The people who despise God's commandments have "come out of the closet," while God's Ten Commandments are being locked away into the closet. As a result our young people who do not receive biblical training have no eternal purpose for their lives. They don't know how to establish faithfully loving, lasting families. They live in a state of confusion about how to be a happy family raising children. They do not know God's promise:

> *"Believe on the Lord Jesus Christ and you will be saved, you and your household* **[your family]***."* Acts 16:31

Our "Egypt" is this present sinful world, ***"under the rule of the Evil One,"*** [48] with all its lies to seduce us into disobedience and destruction. America is plagued with babies born out of wedlock. The incidents of drug abuse and sexual diseases are rising among our youth. There is a great need for parents to teach their young people to abstain from sexual activity until marriage. It is within holy marriage in the presence of God that couples own up to their responsibility to become self-sacrificing fathers and mothers of children.

God's beloved Son, the holy Lamb of God, gave Himself for us to set us free from our sinful fleshly cravings. Through the miraculous work of His Holy Spirit in our hearts Jesus our King enables us to say "NO" to the Evil One and his temptations and to live lives pleasing to God . As we build up one another to live according to His teaching in the Bible, we have the assurance that – when Jesus, the King comes to judge the world — we will not be condemned with the unbelievers.[49] Our faith in God is more powerful than the rule of the "Evil One:"

> *"Who is he who overcomes the world, but he who*

believes that Jesus is the Son of God?" 1 John 5:5

We believe the words of the God who had promised Abraham that He would be his God and the God of Isaac and the God of Jacob and all their children forever. By His faithfulness to them He saved them from "the destroyer" during the plagues in Egypt. He preserved them as one nation through their stay in that land. Then He enabled *"Moses, the servant of the Lord,"*[50] to lead out of Egypt all the descendants of Jacob's twelve sons by their family groups. They started out with God's promise in their hearts that He would lead them back to the land that He had promised to their fore-fathers, Abraham, Isaac and Jacob. This same great Lord God of Israel offers to be the God of every family on earth.

When they arrived at the Red Sea the Egyptian army was pursuing them. It seemed impossible that they could cross the Sea to the other side. But God was with them and He opened it up for them so they could pass through it on dry ground. Then he closed the waves as the Egyptian army followed them on the same ground in their chariots to kill them. This is how God established His honor over Pharaoh and over all his army to show the Egyptians may know that He is the Lord.[51] Moses and the children of Israel were amazed at what God had done for them and they sang a song of praise and joy to their great God.[52]

On their way back to their land, in the fearful wilderness God gave His people manna from heaven for their hunger and gave them water from the Rock for their thirst.[53]

In the wilderness, through Moses, God gave His people the Ten

Commandments,[54] whereby they would be able to live successfully in peace with God and with one another in a lasting society.

The early Americans understood what a treasure we have in the Ten Commandments. All the citizens were expected to live by them and all the children were taught to know them and to observe them. The Ten Commandments were posted in the schools and in public places. The early Americans understood that "United Under God We Stand!"

After having given His people the Ten Commandments in the wilderness God gave Moses this command:

"Let the children of Israel make Me a sanctuary,
that I may dwell among them." Exodus 25:8

This was the command to build *"the tabernacle of meeting,"* [55] a portable tent where God's people were to gather together to meet with God. He gave specific instructions for its construction and for the acceptable manner in which they were to worship Him. God invited everyone of a willing heart to bring to Him offerings for the construction of His sanctuary. It was to be an earthly fore-picture of the promised Messiah-Savior who would come to live among His people to save them from their sin.[56] In the tabernacle God visibly showed His people His Holy Presence in their midst.[57]

When God's beloved Son came to earth the apostle John wrote that in Jesus he himself saw the same glory that the children of Israel have seen in the glory of God displayed in the tabernacle:

>*"And the Word became flesh and dwelt among us, and we beheld His glory as of the only begotten of the Father, full of grace and truth . . .*
>
>*And of His fullness we have all received and grace for grace."* John 1:14, 16

"God's Word" in Jesus came to "set up God's tabernacle," His Presence among us. Even today God is searching for willing hearts and willing families who would invite Him inside so He can display His glory in their midst. The Lord God is calling to us from the Old Testament:

>*"Open up, O ancient gates, and let the King of Glory in.*
>
>*Who is this King of Glory? The Lord strong and mighty, invincible in battle.*
>
>*Yes, open wide the gates and let the King of Glory in.*
>
>*Who is this King of Glory? The Commander of heaven's armies!"* Psalm 24:7-10 Living Bible

The King of Glory is calling us to let Him into our midst so He can establish us into loving, united families. He has the wisdom to make our houses into happy homes. He has the power over the "Evil One" who works among us to turn us against one another. The Lord Jesus has the power to give us forgiving hearts so we can settle our differences with peaceful words. He gives us wisdom to recognize that our conflict is not against one another but against the seductions of the ***"Evil One."*** As — together — we submit to God, the ***"Evil One"*** flees from us.[58] Unbelievers — who come among us — sense God's presence in our midst. They know that we are speaking God's message and they are convicted of the sinful secrets of their heart. Our unity in God is our glory to show the unbelievers their need of God.[59]

As God's people approached the land to which God was leading them, Moses' work among them was done. He went up alone into a mountain where God showed him the Promised Land. Moses, ***"whom the Lord knew face to face"*** died there in fellowship with God. No one knows where he died, for God buried him.[60]

Then God called Joshua to lead the Israelites into the Promised Land. As they were entering the land, Jericho was the first enemy city to be overcome. We have a beautiful example there of how a family was saved because one of its members pleaded for God's mercy on them.

God's mercy toward one enemy family

Among the enemy to be overcome God showed His mercy on one who loved her family. She is Rahab, a harlot of Jericho. Her story is an example of the heart-warming way whereby God is willing to show His mercy on people whom we would consider undeserving. She hid the two Jewish spies who came into the city secretly with this plea for her family:

> *"I know that the Lord has given you the land, that the terror of you has fallen on us . . .*
>
> *As soon as we heard these things* [the miracles the Lord has done for you when you came out of Egypt] *our hearts melted; neither did there remain any more courage in anyone because of you, for the Lord God, He is God in heaven above and on earth beneath.*
>
> *Now therefore, I beg you, swear to me by the Lord, since I have shown you kindness, that you will show kindness to my father's house, and give me a true token,*
>
> *And spare my father, my mother, my brothers, my sisters, and all that they have, and deliver our lives from death."* Joshua 2:2-13

The spies promised to be kind to Rahab and to all her loved ones, even though they were Gentiles, a family of "enemy aliens." They heard her plea for their safekeeping. The spies bound their promise to Rahab to this condition:

> *". . . when we come into the land, you bind this line of scarlet* **[red]** *cord in the window . . . and if you bring your father, your mother, your brothers and all your father's household to your own home.*
>
> *So it shall be that whoever goes outside the doors of your house into the street, his blood shall be on his own head, and we will be guiltless. And whoever is with you in the house, his blood shall be on our head if a hand is laid on him."* Joshua 2:17-19

This historical example proves to us that the God of the Bible is the God of all families. Rahab, a harlot among God's enemies, pleaded safekeeping for her family and God put it into the heart of His men to show compassion toward her plea. The only way the family could be kept safe in the crumbling city if they would stay together inside the one house that God would spare.

When the walls of Jericho came crumbling down at the shout of the children of Israel and they rushed in to destroy the city . . . the two spies went into Rahab's house and safely brought her out, her father, her mother, her brothers and all her relatives. The men spared Rahab, the harlot and all her family *"because she hid the messengers whom Joshua sent to spy out Jericho."* [61] She expressed her faith in the God of the Jews by helping His people.

Rahab's name is listed in the Gospel of Matthew, in the genealogy of the Lord Jesus Christ as one of His great-great-great grandmothers.[62]

The importance of families in God's Book shows again in the way the children of Israel settled the Promised Land after they conquered it. The details are described in the Book of Joshua chapters 13-21. Over and over these words are repeated together with the name of the father of each tribe: *"The father's inheritance was given to them according to their families."* God's dealings were always with the father and his children, "according to his family." God's promises are to you and to your children.

> *"So Joshua took the whole land according to all that the Lord God had said to Moses; and Joshua gave it as an inheritance to Israel according to their divisions by their tribes* **[according to their family groups.]** *Then the land rested from war."* Joshua 11:23

The account ends with a challenge from Joshua to the fathers of the Israelite families:

> *". . .choose for yourselves this day whom you will serve . . .other gods or the Lord . . .But as for me and my house* **[my family]** *we will serve the Lord."* Joshua 24:15

Joshua's heart was set on "family obedience." This is the example our son David pledged to follow. God had chosen Joshua, exemplary father, to lead His people back into the land that God had promised them. But after the people were comfortably settled they began turning to other gods. Joshua's obedience to God was his authority to confront all the other fathers with the fact that they have come to a turning point. Even though some among them chose to worship other gods, Joshua would obey the Lord God of Israel. He would not give in to peer pressure, no matter what direction the others would choose. He and his family would walk according to God's Word!

What direction are the men in America choosing today? How can they choose the only true God and His way if they do not know God's Word?

America needs godly fathers! America needs godly fathers who build a godly next generation on the great godly heritage left behind by our founding fathers. America needs men who are willing to keep themselves pure until marriage, so that they can become strong, self-disciplined leaders of families. America needs men like Joshua whose hearts are set on instructing their children to know and obey God's Word. In our godless public educational institutions our young people learn that they can be wise and good without God. But this is impossible. The time has come for an outcry by ***"the church of the living God, the pillar and foundation of the truth"*** [63] against the people of "the Evil One" who are working to rob America from our Judeo-Christian heritage, the knowledge of God and His Word. Our families and our schools must return to the godly training of our children!

God set up a king over His people

God set up a king over the families of His people. After His people were settled in the land God chose King David, "the man after God's own heart," [64] to rule His people. King David had great joy knowing the God of his forefathers as his God. He desired to honor Him by replacing the simple wilderness-tent-tabernacle of worship with a magnificent stone temple to be built in Jerusalem to the glory of God. But God had a surprise for him. In 2 Samuel 7:1-17 we read:

> *"The word of the Lord came to Nathan the prophet, saying,*
> *"Go, tell My servant David, "Thus says the Lord: Would you build a house for Me to dwell in?*
> *The Lord tells you that He will build you a house.*
> *When your days are fulfilled and you rest with your fathers, I will set up your Seed after you, who will come from your own body, and I will establish His kingdom.*
> *He shall build a house* [a family] *for My name and I will establish the throne of His kingdom forever.*
> *I will be His Father and He shall My Son . . .*
> *And your house and your kingdom shall be established forever before you. Your throne shall be established forever . . ."*

With these words God called King David to stop and think! David had been a man of war. Would he be able to build a peaceful place for God? Would he be able to build a stone building for God to live in? *"Heaven is God's throne and earth is His footstool!"* [65] No! King David could not and would not build for God! It is God who would build for King David. And what God builds is not a stone building. He creates a God-fearing family from King David's own body. A Son will be born in King David's family, *"the Son of*

47

David." [66] The miraculously born Son of God would be the One who would build that family. This will be the family of loving, obedient children of the heavenly Father. God's Son will sit on the throne of King David and will establish God's kingdom forever.

Hearing these wonderful words concerning the Savior, who would be born from his own body into his family, King David was overwhelmed with gratitude to God. At first he was speechless with joy. Then he prayed the words recorded in 2 Samuel 7:18-29. It is an exemplary prayer to be read in its entirety. At the end King David concluded his prayer as follows:

> *"Now what more can David say to You, O Lord God? . . .*
> *For You have made Your people Israel Your very own people forever; and You, Lord have become their God.*
> *Now, O Lord God, the word which You have spoken concerning Your servant and concerning his house,* **[his family]** *establish it forever and do as You said."*

And, yes, God did keep His promise to King David. Many years after King David's death, when the perfect time for the Savior's birth arrived, "the Son of David" was born in Bethlehem, "the city of David." [67]

His miraculous birth as a baby born to a virgin mother had been foretold by the prophet Isaiah hundreds of years before He came. [68]

God prepared the unmarried young Mary for His birth by sending the angel Gabriel to her with this message:

> " . . . *the angel Gabriel was sent by God . . .to a virgin betrothed to a man whose name was Joseph, of the house of David.*
>
> *.. . . .the angel said to her:*
>
> *"Rejoice, highly favored one, the Lord is with you: Blessed are you among women! . . .*
>
> *Do not be afraid Mary, for you have found favor with God.*
>
> *And behold you will conceive in your womb and bring forth a Son and you shall call His name JESUS.*
>
> *He will be great, and will be called the Son of the Highest, and the Lord God will give Him the throne of His father David.*
>
> *And He will reign over the house of Jacob forever, and of His kingdom there will be no end.*
>
> *Then Mary said to the angel, "How can this be, since I do not know a man?"*
>
> *And the angel answered and said, "The Holy Spirit will come upon you, and the power of the Highest will overshadow you: therefore, also, that Holy One who is to be born will be called the Son of God.*
>
> *For with God nothing shall be impossible.*
>
> *Then Mary said: 'Behold, the maidservant of the Lord! Let it be to me according to your word."* Luke 1:26-38

The Lord God of Israel promised to give the throne of King David to his Seed, the One born from his own body, whose kingdom will never end. The God who promised to be the God of Abraham and of his children from his own body would continue to be the God of all his descendants. And this great God would be the One born as a baby from King David's own body into King David's family. He would have a miraculous birth, without a human father.

When God made the promise to Abraham that Isaac would be born by miracle from his own body, he believed God. When God promised King David that the Son of God, King Jesus would be born from his own body into his own family he prayed: ***"Now, Lord God . . . do as You have said."*** [69] And when the virgin Mary heard the angel announce to her the miraculous work of the Holy Spirit in her own body she answered: ***"Let it be to me according to Your word."*** [70]

How about us? What is our answer to the work of the Holy Spirit in our own body?

When Jesus was born, wise men who studied the stars came from far away, from east to Jerusalem and they asked:

> *"Where is the baby born to be the king of the Jews?*
> *We saw His star when it came up in the east, and we have*
> *come to worship Him."* Matthew 2:1,2 TEV

These wise men understood that this baby would be the One to sit on King David's throne to rule the world forever. How about us? This King of the Jews came down from heaven as a baby to live in our midst. As Man He went to the cross to make us His own with His precious shed blood. Then He returned to His glory to make our own body the temple of the Holy Spirit.[71]

God shed His love on us beyond our comprehension. Each time God allows us to experience suffering we do understand a little more fully the price our Lord Jesus Christ paid to make His home within us. We praise Him and thank Him by a life of good works that He has already prepared for us to do.[72]

The risen King Jesus is not only the King of the Jews, but He is "the Lamb on the throne," [73] in heaven. He will rule the world from the throne of His father David. Around Him a great multitude of all nations will be gathered from all tribes and tongues and peoples to worship Him and sing His praises to Him.[74] He is calling each one of us to join the multitude who love Him. He is worthy to reign by His Holy Spirit over our own body, and our every thought and desire.

God's people rejected their King

Yes! God kept His promise. He sent the promised miraculously born Man, the Son of David, the Son of God, to be the King of

God's family! But His people refused Him:

> *"We will not have this Man to reign over us."*
> Luke 19:14

In our day, here in America we hear the same outcry from citizens — blinded by the Evil One — who do not want King Jesus and His laws to rule them or our nation. Will God allow them to have their way? We stand before a choice. We can care about only our physical needs like Esau did. Or we can give our all for the blessing of God like Jacob did. The Father set up King Jesus over us to bless our families. King Jesus *"will reign over the family of Jacob forever and of His kingdom there will be no end."* [75] The Father is calling us to choose His chosen King to take charge of us and our family. Each one of us have to make the same choice that God placed before His people in Jesus' day. Who will be our King?

> *"Pilate said unto the Jews: 'Behold, your King!'*
> *But they cried out, 'Away with Him, away with Him, crucify*
> *Him!"* John 19:15a

And they "handed Jesus over to the Gentiles to be crucified" just like He had already foretold to His disciples. [76]

> *"As Jesus was going up to Jerusalem he took the twelve disciples aside and spoke to them privately, as they walked along.*
>
> *"Listen," he told them, "we are going up to Jerusalem, where the Son of Man will be handed over to the chief priests and the teachers of the Law. They will condemn him to death and then hand him over to the Gentiles, who will make fun of him, whip him, and nail him to the cross; and on the third day he will be raised to life."*
> Matthew 20:17-19 TEV

> *"For I tell you this: the Scripture that says, 'He was included with the criminals,' must come true about me. For that which was written about me is coming true."*
> Luke 22:37 TEV

The cruelty that the Lord Jesus Christ had to suffer unjustly at the hands of hateful men was already foretold in the Old Testament Scriptures. After His resurrection He appeared to His disciples and taught them how the fulfilled prophecies prove that He is the promised Savior of the world. He said to them:

> *"O foolish ones, and slow of heart to believe all that the prophets have spoken! Ought not the Christ to have suffered these things and to enter into His glory?*
>
> *And beginning at Moses and all the Prophets, He explained to them in all the Scriptures the things* **[the truth]** *concerning Himself. . .*
>
> *And His disciples said to one another, 'Did not our heart burn within us while He talked with us on the road and He opened the Scriptures to us?"* Luke 24:25-32

Whenever we disobey God we are rejecting His rule over us. His heart is grieved every time we sin because we are hurting ourselves. Our own way leads to disaster cutting us off from fellowship with God and with one another. God's people chose to bring this disaster on themselves when God presented Himself before them in Person as a Man. Just like it had been foretold in the Old Testament Scriptures, [77] they nailed Him to a cross. Above His head they posted the written accusation against Him in three languages, Hebrew, Greek and Latin:

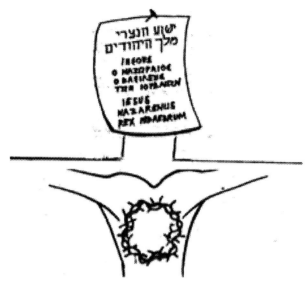

"THIS IS JESUS, THE KING OF THE JEWS." Matthew 27:37

"HAD THE RULERS OF THIS AGE KNOWN THE HIDDEN WISDOM OF GOD, THEY WOULD NOT HAVE CRUCIFIED THE LORD OF GLORY."
1 Corinthians 2:7,8

God raised His King from the dead

But thanks be to God, Jesus, the King of the Jews did not remain dead. God raised Him from the dead just like it was prophesied by the prophets.

To Abraham God promised a Savior,[78] who would bless every family on the earth. To King David God promised that this Savior[79] will be King over every family on earth. Abraham and King David believed that the God who had spoken to them is "the God who raises the dead." King David believed God's promise that He would raise up a family for Himself from King David's descendants and that One from among his descendants would be the King over His family. This Great Descendant would sit on King David's throne to rule God's family forever.[80] King David believed that this great King would be born as a baby into his family and that death would have no power over His body. In Psalm 16 King David foretold the resurrection of this great King more than a thousand years before He was born.

On the day of Pentecost the apostle Peter — filled with the Holy Spirit — preached the resurrection of the crucified King of the Jews. He quoted King David's prophecy from Psalm 16 in these words:

> *"I foresaw the Lord always before my face,*
> *For He is at my right hand, that I may not be shaken,*
> *Therefore my heart rejoiced and my tongue was glad;*
> *Moreover my flesh also will rest in hope,*
> *For You will not leave my soul in Hades,*
> *Nor will You allow Your Holy One to see corruption.*
> *You have made known to me the ways of life;*
> *You will make me full of joy in Your presence."* Acts 2:24-28

God kept His promise to King David. The dead body of "the Son of David," "the Holy One" did not suffer the decay of death, but was raised to new life on the third day. Peter ended his message with this public declaration:

> *"Therefore being exalted to the right hand of God,*
> *and having received from the Father the promise of the*
> *Holy Spirit, He poured out this which you see and hear . . .*
> *Therefore let all the house of Israel know assuredly*
> *that God has made this Jesus, whom you crucified, both*
> *Lord and Christ."* Acts 2:33, 36

To the Steers family the good news of the resurrection of the Lord Jesus Christ, our Savior is very precious. We will never forget that day when we were gathered together with broken hearts at the fresh grave of our loved one, David. The only comfort came from "the God who raises the dead." This unshakeable assurance in God gives the only lasting consolation to any family who is faced with the death of a loved one.

God conquers the hearts of His people

God promises to conquer the rebellious hearts of His people. The Lord God of Israel kept renewing His promise of mercy to His people even though throughout their history again and again the descendants of Jacob *"tempted God and limited the Holy One of Israel and did not believe His wondrous works . . .*[81] His offer of forgiveness never changed even when He had to allow the enemy to invade their land and to burn their temple and to carry them away captives into foreign lands.[82]

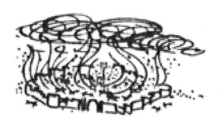

The Lord God of the Bible is *"a consuming fire, a jealous God."*[83] But He is always ready to receive back to Himself those who turn to Him in repentance. He enabled His people to rebuild their temple twice, but then — after the crucifixion of their Messiah — in 70 AD the Romans destroyed it. The Jews have been dispersed all over the world for more than two thousand years. In foreign lands they experienced God's anger, just like Moses had warned them of it.[84] In 1948 finally, by a miracle of God the land of Israel was returned to the Jews. But officially they are still rejecting their Messiah. Their temple is still in ruins. Next to its ruins a Muslim Mosque stands on Mount Zion.

In America many families and many lives are in ruins, because of the seductions of "the thief," the "Evil One," who works to keep them ignorant of God's Word. But God never changed His mind concerning His promise of His mercy toward all of us. Through the prophet Ezekiel He promised His people to give them a new heart, a heart filled with cheerful willingness to obey Him. He offers this miracle to any willing heart among any people anywhere in the world:

> *"I had concern for My holy name, which the house of Israel had profaned among the nations wherever they went.*
>
> *Therefore say to the house of Israel, 'Thus says the Lord God: 'I do not do this for your sake, O house of Israel but for My holy name's sake, which you have profaned among the nations wherever you went.*
>
> *And I will sanctify My great name, which has been profaned among the nations, which you have profaned in their midst, and the nations shall know that I AM the Lord,' says the Lord God, 'when I am hallowed in you before their eyes.'*
>
> *For I will take you from among the nations, gather you out of all the countries and bring you into your own land.*
>
> *Then I will sprinkle clean water on you, I will cleanse you from all your filthiness and from all your idols.*
>
> *I will give you a new heart and a new Spirit within you. I will take the heart of stone out of your flesh and give you a heart of flesh* **[a heart of love]**.
>
> *I will put My Spirit within you and cause you to walk in My statutes and you will keep My judgments and do them.*
>
> *. . . you shall be My people and I will be your God. I will deliver you from all your uncleanness . . .*
>
> *Not for your sake do I do this,' says the Lord God, 'let it be known to you. Be ashamed and confounded for your own ways, O house of Israel . . .*
>
> *Then the nations which are left all around you shall know that I the Lord, have rebuilt the ruined places and planted what was desolate, the Lord have spoken it,*

and I will do it.

Thus says the Lord God: I will also let the house of Israel inquire of Me to do this for them: I will increase their men like a flock.

Like a flock offered as holy sacrifices, like the flock at Jerusalem on its feast days, so shall the ruined cities be filled with flocks of men.

Then they shall know that I AM the Lord." Ezekiel 36:21-38

"They shall be My people and I will be their God;

then I will give them one heart and one way, that they may fear Me forever, for the good of them and their children after them.

And I will make an everlasting covenant with them, that I will not

turn away from doing them good; but I will put My fear in their hearts so that they will not depart from Me." Jeremiah 32:39

Notice again these words: **". . . for the good of them and their children after them."** No human being could accomplish this miraculous transforming work in stubborn human hearts, but the heavenly Father's own beloved Son can do it. All parents who have raised children know that they come into the world with a strong will, demanding their own way. All children have a bent toward evil and have to be taught to be good. If they are not disciplined they get out of hand and bring shame and grief to their parents. Our sinful nature is our problem, not lack of money or lack of jobs or bad economy. Our bent toward evil is our problem. God cannot bless a people who disobey His Word!

From the beginning of mankind, and throughout the history of the Jewish people, the promised coming of "the Messiah-Savior" was the heartfelt comfort and joy of all who believed God's good news for "you and your children." All parents need to fix their hearts on God's promise:

"The Deliverer will come out of Zion, and He will turn away ungodliness from Jacob [and his children].

For this is my covenant with them, when I take away their sins." Romans 11:27

The God of the Bible will prove to the whole world that He is the God Most High. He proves to us that He is good because He teaches us sinful people His way.[85] He promises to work mightily in the hearts of our children through His Holy Spirit as we faithfully discipline them and teach them His life-giving Word:

"Therefore thus says the Lord who redeemed Abraham, concerning the house of Jacob:

Jacob shall not now be ashamed, nor shall his face grow pale, but when he sees his children, the work of My hands, in his midst,

They will sanctify My name, and sanctify the Holy One of Jacob, and fear the God of Israel.

Those also who erred in spirit will come to understanding, and those who complained will learn doctrine."
Isaiah 29:22-24

"When Jacob sees his children, the work of My hands in his midst." Over and over again in the Bible God declares that He is willing and able to transform rebellious human hearts into obedient hearts:

"Yet hear now, O Jacob My servant, and Israel whom I have chosen.

Thus says the Lord who made you and formed you from the womb, who will help you.

Fear not, O Jacob My servant, and you . . . whom I have chosen, for I will pour water on him who is thirsty . . . I will pour My Spirit on your descendants and My blessing on your offspring . . .

Remember these, O Jacob, and Israel, for you are My servant, I have formed you, you are My servant, O

Israel, you will not be forgotten by Me!
I have blotted out, like a thick cloud, your trans-
gressions, and like a cloud your sins . . .
Sing, O heavens, for the Lord has done it . . .
For the Lord has redeemed Jacob, and glorified
Himself in Israel." Isaiah 44:1-3, 21-23

"I will pour out My Spirit on your descendants and My blessing on your children." The God of Jacob is our God and our children's God. God's promises are always "to you and to your children." He is waiting for us to come to Him and tell Him that we will trust Him.

"Be still and know that I am God. I will be exalted
among the nations, I will be exalted in the earth!
The Lord of hosts is with us, the God of Jacob is
our refuge." Psalm 46:10, 11

All nations are made up of family groups. How wonderful it is to have "the God of Jacob" as our refuge for our families. As we turn to Revelation chapter 7, we see what God does according to His promises in this passage with His family, the twelve sons of Jacob:

One hundred and forty four thousand Israelites, twelve thousand of all the tribes, the family groups of the children of Israel are sealed to be the first fruits of the heavenly city, the

New Jerusalem.

All the names listed are of Jacob's family — with their families.

Did God keep them a nation while they were in Egypt for four hundred years?

Did He bring them out complete with families?

Did God keep them a nation during 2000 years while they were scattered among the other nations of earth?

Did He keep them through the cruel Nazi Holocaust?

Are they now back in their promised land by miracle?

Our risen Lord Jesus Christ offers the same blessing of His keeping power to us Gentiles, to our families.

God gives us many difficult lessons to learn in this life. It takes sacrifice and selflessness for families to learn to live together in love and unity. But our heavenly Father teaches us to really enjoy one another as we — together — set our hearts on His promises. Then He gives us — together –- the assurance that He is pleased with us. As we put His Word into action we have the joy of knowing that He is spreading His blessing to others through us. He is faithful to His promise:

> *"I will give you the sure mercies that I gave David."*
Acts 13:34

The King of the Jews, everyone's Savior

The King of the Jews is the Savior of everyone in the whole world. Before Jesus came into the world, the Father made this promise to His beloved Son:

> *"It is too small a thing that You should be My Servant to*
> *raise the tribes of Jacob, and to restore the preserved ones of Israel.*
> *I will also give You as a light to the Gentiles, That You should be My salvation to the ends of the earth."*
> Isaiah 49:6

Jesus is the great King whose name shall be honored among all nations. Even though at this present time the great temple of King David's dream is in ruins, God did not forget the promise that He had made to him about building him a God-honoring family:

> *"God at the first visited the Gentiles to take out of them a people for His name,*
> *and with this the words of the prophets agree just as it is written:*
> *After this I will return and rebuild the tabernacle of David, which is fallen down;*

I will rebuild its ruins and I will set it up.
So that the rest of mankind may seek the Lord,
Even all the Gentiles who are called by My name,
says the Lord, who does all these wonders.
Known to God from eternity are all His works."
Acts 15:14-18

"I will return and rebuild the tabernacle of David, which is fallen down." God heard King David's prayer for a Temple of worship, "a house of prayer," to be set up in Jerusalem to honor the God of his fore-fathers. But the tabernacle that God is rebuilding is not a stone building and it is not merely in Jerusalem. God visited the Gentiles to call from among them people who seek Him and love Him and worship Him all over the world:

"For I tell you that Christ became a Servant of the Jews to show you that God is faithful to make His promises to the patriarchs **[fore-fathers]** *come true and also to enable the Gentiles to praise God for His mercy. As the Scripture says: . . .*
Rejoice, you Gentiles, with God's chosen people!"
Romans 15:8-10

"We are His workmanship created in Christ Jesus for good works, which God prepared beforehand that we should walk in them." Ephesians 2:10

"You are . . . the sons of the covenant which God made with our fathers, saying to Abraham: 'And in your Seed all the families of the earth shall be blessed.'
To you first, God, having raised up His Servant Jesus, sent Him to bless you **[your family]** *in turning away every one of you from your iniquities."* Acts 3:25, 26

"The works of the Lord are great, studied by all who have pleasure in them. The works of the Lord are honorable and glorious, . .

He will ever be mindful of His covenant . . .
Holy and awesome is His name." Psalm 111:2,3,5

God sent His Son to bless us in our families by turning each one of us away from our sin. Saving us from our sin is God's first purpose for our lives whether in sorrow or in joy.

The New Covenant sealed by Jesus' blood

Oh, what heartfelt comfort and joy we experience as we, so prone to sin, remember Jesus' promise at His last supper before His death.

He took the bread, blessed and broke it and gave it to the disciples saying:

> *"Take, eat, this is My body.'*
> *Then He took the cup, and gave thanks, and gave it*
> *to them, saying: 'Drink from it, all of you.*
> *For this is My blood of the new covenant, which is*
> *shed for many for the remission of sins.*
> *But I say to you, I will not drink of this fruit of the*
> *vine from now on until that day when I drink it new with*
> *you in My Father's kingdom."*
> Mathew 26:26-28

This New Covenant was foretold by the prophets Ezekiel and Jeremiah and they have already been quoted a few pages ago in this book. Through His prophets God promises that He Himself would put the desire to obey Him into our hearts. God is faithful to keep His promises made to the fore-fathers. We, the believing Gentiles are Abraham's descendants and we are included into the promises that God made to him and his offspring.[86] As by faith we partake of Jesus' crucified body, pictured in the broken bread and His precious shed blood, pictured in the vine in the cup, we remember our Lord on the cross dieing for our sin. On the cross He took our sinful self with Him into His death and now — as our risen Lord — He is raising us to the new life of obedience to the Father, according to His Word:

> *"I will make a new covenant with the house of Israel and with the house of Judah* [**Jacob's descendants**].
> *For this is the covenant that I will make with the house of Israel after those days, says the Lord, I will put My laws in their mind and write them on their hearts and I will be their God and they shall be My people."* Hebrews 8:10, see also Hebrews 10:12-18, Jeremiah 32:39-42

All who believe in Jesus, no matter what nationality, all are invited to partake of the Lord's Supper by eating that bread and drinking that cup. Together we proclaim the Lord's death for us, His forgiving love poured down on us. Together we yield ourselves to His cleansing work in our hearts and lives so that He will save us from having to be condemned with the unbelieving world.[87] Together we proclaim our faith in His coming for us in His glory.

His coming in glory is more than His coming for us. It is also His victory over "the Evil One." Jesus knew that it will serve His glory even when Judas, the traitor, slipped out from the Last Supper into the night with Satan in his heart. Judas went out to sell Jesus into the hands of His enemies for thirty pieces of silver. As Jesus watched him leave He exclaimed:

> *"Now the Son of man is glorified and God is glorified in Him."* John 13:31

The Lord Jesus knew that when He would be lifted up on His cross, He would overthrow "the Evil One." He would draw people to come to Himself, their Creator and Lord and He would set them free from the clutches of "the thief." [88]

We Gentiles, who have been drawn in repentance to the crucified Lord of glory, we inherit Abraham's blessing, "I am your God and I am your children's God forever." This is the blessing we pass on to our children. And in the Lord Jesus Christ we inherit the same Presence of God freely given to the believing fore-fathers. This blessing is the Holy Spirit freely poured out on us, too:

> *"Christ has redeemed us from the curse of the law, having become a curse for us . . .that the blessing of Abraham might come upon the Gentiles in Christ Jesus, that we might <u>receive the promise of the Holy Spirit through faith</u>.*
> *. . . Now to Abraham and his Seed were the promises made. He does not say, "And to your seeds," as of many, but as of one, "and to your Seed," who is Christ."*
> Galatians 3:13-16; Genesis 15:4 (with emphasis)

This is the promise that our son David kept bringing to my attention in his last letter: "Remember, Mom, the Holy Spirit is <u>to you and</u> <u>to your children. Acts 2:39."</u>

> *"Thanks be to God who gives us the victory through our Lord Jesus Christ."*
> 1 Corinthians 15:57

Heirs of Abraham's blessing

The biblical family of any nationality inherits the blessing of Abraham. Again, let us meditate on Peter's words at Pentecost concerning our children:

> *"Repent and let every one of you be baptized in the name of Jesus Christ for the remission of sins and you*

shall receive the gift of the Holy_Spirit.
For the promise is to you and to your children and to all who are afar off, as many as the Lord our God will call." Acts 2:38, 39

The promise of the Holy Spirit is to any repentant individual, or couple or family. Paul and Silas preached this same good news to the keeper of the prison when the earthquake popped the doors open:

"Believe on the Lord Jesus Christ and you will be saved, you and your family." Acts 16:31 (with emphasis)

Jesus saves us from God's wrath that is to come on the disobedient. God offers His mercies to all who set their heart on His blessing as the fore-fathers did. Cornelius, a centurion of the Roman army stationed in Israel, recognized with all his household that the God of the Jews is the one true God and longed for His blessing on his family. God sent an angel to give him this instruction:

"Call for Simon whose surname is Peter, for he will tell you words by which you and all your household [your family] will be saved." Acts 11:14

Cornelius obeyed the angel's instruction and sent for Peter. When he arrived Cornelius and his whole household were gathered together eagerly waiting to hear what Peter would have to say:

"Cornelius said: '. . . you have done well to come. Now therefore, we are all present before God, to hear all the things commanded you by God.'
Then Peter opened his mouth and said:
'In truth I perceive that God shows no partiality.
But in every nation whoever fears Him and works righteousness is accepted by Him.
The word which God sent to the children of Israel, preaching peace through Jesus Christ: He is Lord

of all — . . .

That word you know . . . how God anointed Jesus of Nazareth with the Holy Spirit and with power, who went about doing good and healing all who were oppressed by the devil, for God was with Him . . .

Whom they killed by hanging on a tree.

Him God raised up on the third day and showed Him openly,

Not to all people, but to witnesses chosen before by God, even to us who ate and drank with Him after He arose from the dead.

And He commanded us to preach to the people, and to testify that it is He who was ordained by God to be the Judge of the living and the dead.

To Him all the prophets witness that, through His name, whoever believes in Him will receive remission **[forgiveness]** *of sins.*" Acts 10:33-43

When Peter returned to Jerusalem the apostles and brethren gathered together to demand an explanation of why he had gone to visit Gentiles, since this was forbidden to circumcised Jewish people. Peter explained to them how God commanded him to visit Cornelius and then added these words:

"As I began to speak the Holy Spirit fell upon them, as upon us at the beginning.

Then I remembered the word of the Lord Jesus how He had said:

'John indeed baptized with water, but you shall be baptized with the Holy Spirit.'

. . . When they **[the brethren]** *heard these things they became silent; and they glorified God, saying: 'Then God has also granted to the Gentiles repentance to life."*
Acts 11:14-18

While Peter was explaining who the Lord Jesus is to Cornelius' household, they believed his words and the Holy Spirit filled their hearts in the same way as He had done to the first disciples on the first Sunday of Pentecost.[89] We will experience the same miracle as we learn to live according to God's great love toward us and toward all people. Then He enables us to share with others *"the good news promised long ago by God through His prophets, and written in the Holy Scriptures about our Lord Jesus Christ."* [90] The Holy Spirit will work in the hearts of those who hear us and will bring them to faith in Jesus.

All nations are made up of family groups. The Jewish people are not the only family group for whom God's Son died. Hear the prophecy spoken when Jesus raised Lazarus from the dead:

> *"And one of them, Caiaphas, being high priest that year said to them, 'You know nothing at all, nor do you consider that it is expedient for us that one man should die for the people, and not that the whole nation should perish.*
>
> *Now this he did not say on his own authority, but being high priest that year he prophesied that Jesus would die for the Jewish nation.*
>
> *And not for that nation only, but also that He would gather together in one <u>all the children of God</u> who were scattered abroad."* John 11:49-52 (with emphasis)

God sent His beloved Son to die for all the children of God of every nation. He is building that family which He promised to King David. He is gathering us out from among the unbelievers into one family of loving children to the heavenly Father who are learning to obey Him according to His written Word.

Yes, God's Son is mindful of His New Covenant to do His miraculous works whereby He works His own obedience into our hearts. He hears our prayers for obedience for ourselves and for our children:

> *"For the mercy of the Lord is from everlasting to everlasting on those who fear Him, and His righteousness to <u>children's children,</u>*
> *to such as keep His covenant and to those who remember His commandments to do them."* Psalm 103:17, 18 (with emphasis)

God's mercies are to those who "keep His covenant," who obey His commandments, not depending on themselves, but on His promise that He Himself works in us to will and to do His good pleasure.[91] And even if there is only one believer in the family, the whole family is holy to the Lord:

> *"The unbelieving husband is made acceptable to God by being united to his wife, and the unbelieving wife is made acceptable to God by being united to her Christian husband. If this were not so, their children would be like pagan children; but as it is, they are acceptable to God."* 1 Corinthians 7:14 TEV

> *"Blessed is the man who fears the Lord, who delights greatly in His commandments, His descendants shall be mighty on earth. The generation of the upright will be blessed."* Ps. 112:1, 2

"Ask and you shall receive" [92]

At the time when the Lord Jesus Christ was on earth the majestic Temple of Jerusalem, the dream of King David, was rebuilt and it was standing as a great attraction for the whole world. It is that Temple which the Lord Jesus entered with holy indignation. He made a whip from cords and cleansed the Temple by driving out the animals and overturning the tables of the money-changers. He gave this command:

"Do not make <u>My Father's house</u> a market place!"
John 2:16

"It is written in the Scriptures that God said, 'My house will be called <u>a house of prayer for all nations</u>."
Mark 11:17

"His disciples remembered that the Scripture says, 'My zeal for Your house [**your family**] *O God, burns in Me like fire."* John 2:17

Jesus' fiery devotion did not burn for a building, but He was concerned about what God's children, "the Father's household," were doing in the Temple of worship. He called the place of worship "My Father's house." His action of cleansing the Temple is symbolic of His work in our hearts and in our families when He convicts us of our sin.[93] He declared that His Father's family should be a "family of prayer." At times — even now — our Lord Jesus has to take out His whip to get us down on our knees in prayer.

> *"Therefore My people shall know My name, therefore they shall know in that day that I am He who speaks, behold it is I."* Isaiah 52:6

Jesus paid a price — beyond our comprehension — for our prayers. At the moment when Jesus died for our sin on the cross, the curtain of the Temple that kept sinful people out of God's Holy Presence, was ripped in two.[94] That veil is symbolic of His body. By one perfect sacrifice for our sin, His crucified body and His shed blood, He opened up for us, sinful people, the new and living way into God's holiest Presence. He is now at right hand of the Father as our great High Priest whose one perfect sacrifice for the forgiveness of our sin entitles us to come boldly with our prayers to the throne of grace.[95]

Jesus is calling us — anyone, anywhere — to come to the Father in prayer and ask Him: "Father, do to me, too, as You have said! Pour down on me and my loved ones the sure mercies that You have promised to King David and to Your people Israel and to anyone who comes and asks You for them." The God of the Bible is ready to make Himself known to us even as He did to King David and to our fore-fathers in the faith. As we come to Him in prayer He teaches us to enjoy His Holy Presence through His Holy Spirit:

> *"Everyone who holds fast My covenant . . . I will bring them to My holy mountain and make them joyful in My house of prayer.*
> *Their burnt offerings and their sacrifices will be accepted on My altar, For My house* **[the Father's family]**

70

<u>*shall be called a house of prayer for all nations.*</u>" Isaiah 56:7
(emphasis added)

The heavenly Father's family is to be a family united in prayer. Our great High Priest, Jesus Christ at the right of the Father is waiting for us to come to the Father in prayer. He is glorified in us as we come to the throne of grace praying the way He taught us to pray: ***"Our Father in heaven, hallowed be Your name. Your kingdom come, Your will be done on earth as it is in heaven."*** [96] This is the way He prayed in the Garden of Gethsemane before He went to the cross in obedience to the Father.

<u>"God's house" is His family</u>

When God speaks of His house He speaks of His family, His household.

" . . . *the house of God . . . is the church of the living God, the pillar and the foundation of the truth.*" 1 Timothy 3:15b

When God speaks of His household He speaks of His family, the Church. We are cooperating with the Lord Jesus each time we faithfully gather together ***"with one accord in one place,"*** [97] in order to worship the God of the Bible. Every Sunday or during the week as we assemble with others to seek God in His written Word, we are building with God the family that He had promised to King David. God gives us the assurance that He is pleased with us as we pray together to Him for enabling grace to live in obedience to His written Word. He is working in our hearts and lives according to His promise:

> *"I will glorify the house of My glory . . . To bring your sons from afar. . . to the name of the Lord your God and to the Holy One of Israel, because He has glorified you."* Isaiah 60:7c, 9

> *"If you then, being evil, know how to give good gifts to your children, how much more will your heavenly Father give the Holy Spirit to those who ask Him.!"* Luke 11:13

> *"For the Son of God, Jesus Christ, who was preached among you by us . . . was not Yes and No, but in Him was YES,*
> *For all the promises of God in Him are YES and in Him Amen, to the glory of God through us."* 2 Corinthians 1:19, 20

We bring pleasure to God when we say our "YES," our "So be it" to His promises:

> *"And My elect shall long enjoy the work of their hands,*
> *They shall not labor in vain, nor bring forth children for trouble, for they shall be the descendants of the blessed of the Lord, and their children with them.*
> *It shall come to pass that before they call, I will answer, and while they are still speaking, I will hear."* Isaiah 65:23, 24

Notice again that "the blessed of the Lord," are those parents who raise their children for His pleasure with sacrificial work and prayer. They can count on God to include their children into His blessing. Even before we start to pray He has already heard our heart-cry for them.

And God hears the prayers of anyone, any childless person or couple, also, who are prayerfully doing sacrificial, self-giving work to pass on His blessing to those in need. Whoever does any kindness in Jesus' name to anyone in need , Jesus counts that deed as having been done to Him.[98]

Kneel at the Cross, Jesus will meet you there

The Father hears our prayers because of what His Son did for us on the cross. During His peoples wanderings through the fearful wilderness God gave them a preview of Jesus' crucifixion at the entrance of the tabernacle. He commanded them to offer to Him there a continual whole burnt offering, a "holocaust" [99] of a lamb on the altar, a pleasing fragrance to God:

>*"One lamb in the morning and the other lamb you shall offer at twilight. . . . a sweet aroma, an offering made by fire to the Lord.*
>
>*This shall be a continual burnt offering throughout your generations at the door of the tabernacle of meeting before the Lord,*
>
>*Where I will meet you to speak with you there.*
>
>*And there I will meet with the children of Israel, and the tabernacle shall be sanctified by My glory.*
>
>*So I will consecrate the tabernacle of meeting and the altar.*
>
>*I will also consecrate both Aaron and his sons to minister to Me as priests.*
>
>*I will dwell among the children of Israel and will be their God.*
>
>*And they shall know that I am the Lord their God who brought them up out of the land of Egypt that I may dwell among them. I am the Lord their God."* Exodus 29:38-46
>(emphasis added)

Our perfect Lamb has already been sacrificed on God's altar. Jesus, our Lamb, not only died, but rose again from the dead. He shall make known to us that He has delivered us from our Egypt, the unbelieving world where He is being rejected. And He has brought us in among His disciples among whom we are being made into a family of loving, obedient children to the heavenly Father. To us, who long for God to live in our hearts and in our midst, the Lord Jesus explains how to enjoy the blessing of His continual Presence:

> *"Whoever loves Me will obey My message. My Father will love him and My Father and I will come to him and live with him."* John 14: 23 TEV

God Himself makes His home with His people who love Him and live according to His Word. He is the God who hears and answers the prayers that are said according to His will.[100] The Bible teaches us that our prayers rise up to God like the sweet fragrance of burning incense.[101] God richly pours down His free gift of enabling grace on those for whom we pray and He is being glorified when we thank Him for His answers to our prayers.[102]

> *"Thanks be to God for His indescribable gift."* 2 Corinthians 9:15 TEV

<u>Teach your children</u>

The older generation makes God known to the next generation. Sadly, if the older generation does not know God from the Bible, they leave behind the image of a false god for their children. They leave behind disappointment, confusion and hopelessness for their offspring.

For this reason God commands each older generation to make Him known according to His written Word from generation to generation:

> *"That which our fathers have told us we will not hide from their children, telling to the generation to come the praises of the Lord,*
>
> *And His strength and His wonderful works that He has done.*
>
> *For He established a testimony in Jacob, and appointed a law in Israel,*
>
> *Which He commanded our fathers, that they should make them known to their children, that the generation to come might know them, the children that should be born.*
>
> *That they may arise and declare them to their children,*
>
> *That they may set their hope in God and not forget the works of God, but keep His commandments,*
>
> *And may not be like their fathers, a stubborn and rebellious generation, a generation that did not set their heart aright,*
>
> *Whose spirit was not faithful to God."* Psalm 78:1-8

As the parents and grandparents express their faith in God the children will see from their lives how wonderfully God worked in them. The children will know that they have been trained by their parents according to God's wisdom. They will experience God's blessing of love and unity on their family. Then the children will also want to know God and to obey Him. God Himself will convince the young people of how His truth had good results in their family.[103] When the children hear their parents praising God they will not become rebellious.

Oh, if only the men of America and the men of the whole world would know what a privilege it is to be a father of a family, a father after God's own heart! If they would know their privilege in God they would not be enslaved to the immoral way of life. They would faithfully love their wife and children. God offers to make men into trustworthy providers and protectors of their families. Such head of families are loved and respected by their wife and children.

When children are taught the Word of God they grow up to be a pleasure to their parents and to be a blessing in their neighborhoods and to all the people around them. As the fathers and mothers speak of how God has worked His kindness in their lives their children become convinced that He is perfectly worthy of their obedience no matter what the cost. Children will honor their father and mother who are training them by loving discipline to live according to God's Word. They will experience what their parents have learned, that God's promises are coming true in their own lives. God promises to those who obey His laws that He will prosper everything they do in His service.[104] When godly parents come to their old age their children will remember how they have been loved throughout their lives. Those children will want to return the love that they have received. Every father is the earthly picture of the heavenly Father.

The key purpose of our lives as parents and grandparents is to prepare our children from God's Word for the coming of our risen Lord Jesus Christ in glory. Our children and all our offspring are our crown of rejoicing in the presence of the Lord at His coming.[105] Our fervent prayer for them is that at the coming of the Lord of glory they all be found as members of the great family that God had promised to King David, by receiving the miraculously born Son of David, the Son of God into their hearts and lives.

Yes, our risen Lord and Savior Jesus Christ is coming back in His glory and every eye shall see Him, even they who crucified Him. Our great God will not allow the "Evil One" and his cohorts to continue endlessly to rule the world with his lies and sorceries and seductions and destructions. Our Lord is coming to judge the world with His truth.[106] When evil multiplies among us, when family members turn against each other betraying each other's trust, when citizens rebel against the government that God has ordained over them, we can call out with Thomas Jefferson:

> "Can the liberties of a nation be thought secure when we have removed their only firm basis, a conviction in the minds of the people that these liberties are the gift of God? That they are not to be violated but with His wrath?
>
> Indeed, I tremble for my country when I reflect that God is just; that His justice cannot sleep forever."[107]

Jesus is coming again

Among His last words to His disciples the Lord Jesus made this promise:

> *"Do not be worried and upset. . . Believe in God, and believe also in Me.*
>
> *There are many rooms in my Father's house, and I am going to prepare a place for you. I would not tell you this if it were not so.*

And after I go and prepare a place for you, I will come back and take you to myself, so that you will be where I am . . .

And because I live, you also will live. . ." John 14:1-3, 19b TEV

While the Lord Jesus prepares a place for us in His Father's house, we are preparing ourselves for that great Day when He comes for us. He declared with very strong words that not everyone will be welcome by His Father:

"Not everyone who says to Me, Lord, Lord, shall enter the kingdom of heaven, but he who does the will of My Father in heaven.
Many will say to Me in that day, Lord, Lord, have we not prophesied in Your name, cast out demons in Your name, and done many wonders in Your name?
And then I will declare to them, 'I never knew you, depart from Me, you, who practice lawlessness." Matthew 7:21-23

The Father of the Lord Jesus Christ welcomes only those who obey His Son. Jesus illustrated these words with the parable of the two houses. Only that person is building his life on the unshakeable Rock who hears and obeys what Jesus says to him.[108] All of us will have to stand before the Father and give an account of how well we have obeyed His Living Word, Jesus, who makes Himself known to us from God's written Word.[109]

Daily, we urgently need each other to exhort and build up one another in our faith.[110] We, ourselves, experienced on September 11, 2001 in the attack on the two towers in New York, how the enemy is ever scheming to attack suddenly and unexpectedly. As the Bible says, the "Evil One" is like a roaring lion always ready to devour those who are not alert of his schemes.[111] "The thief" is ever scheming to rob us of our loving fellowship with God and with one another.

The apostle John exhorts us with these words to prepare ourselves for Jesus' return in glory:

"And now little children, abide in Him, that when He appears we may have confidence and not be ashamed before Him at His coming." 1 John 2:28

Urgently, we need to be in prayer for one another that together we will understand the glory of our great God. His will is to make Himself known to the world through us. He calls us to live according to the good news of His promised blessings resting on us. Here is the prayer that the apostle Paul left behind for us:

"I do not cease to give thanks to God for you in my prayers,

that the God of our Lord Jesus Christ, the Father of glory, may give to you the spirit of wisdom and revelation in the knowledge of Him,

the eyes of your understanding being enlightened, that you may know what is the hope of His calling, what are the riches of the glory of His inheritance in the saints,

and what is the exceeding greatness of His power toward us who believe, according to the working of His mighty power,

which He worked in Christ when He raised Him from the dead and seated Him at His right hand in the heavenly places,

far above all principality and power and might and dominion and every name that is named, not only in this age but also in that which to come.

And He put all things under His feet and He gave Him to be head over all things to the church,

Which is His body, the fullness of Him who fills all in all." Ephesians 1:15-23

Our Father wants each one of us to experience within ourselves that mighty power whereby He raised His beloved Son from the dead. By His miraculous might He wants to raise us from the death of sin to live unto His pleasure, which is impossible by human effort.

Our Father knew that we would have fear in our hearts in this present evil world. We have to face hatred and misunderstandings and persecutions among the people who are rejecting Him or don't yet know Him. We must be rooted in His unspeakable love that He poured out on us while we were still sinners, when His beloved Son went to the cross for our forgiveness. His apostles and many of those saints, our heroes, who preserved the written word of God for us paid a terrible price for what they did. Here is a sample prayer for one another that the apostle Paul left behind for us:

> *"For this reason I bow my knees to the Father of our Lord Jesus Christ,*
> *from whom the whole family in heaven and earth is named,*
> *that He would grant you, according to the riches of His glory, to be strengthened with might through His Spirit in the inner man,*
> *that Christ may dwell in your hearts through faith, that you being rooted and grounded in love,*
> *may be able to comprehend with all the saints what is the width and length and depth and height –*
> *to know the love of Christ which passes knowledge, that you may be filled with all the fullness of God.*
> *Now to Him who is able to do exceedingly abundantly above all that we ask or think, according to the power that works in us,*
> *To Him be glory in the church by Christ Jesus to all generations, forever and ever. Amen."* Ephesians 3:14-21

Our Father's love for us in His beloved Son is mightier than anything that the "Evil One" can do to us in deceiving us and robbing us of our sustaining, loving fellowship with God and with one another.

Individuals, married couples, families,

Individuals, married couples, families, all who live "in the true God" are God's family.

Our son David wrote the following words in his Bible: "We can have great joy in Jesus and we can bring that joy to others." He had the joy of knowing this great and awesome God, the God of the Bible. He left behind his conviction as a loving father of his family that he could entrust his wife and children to this great and awesome God, even now when he is already at home with the Lord. The God of the Bible, the God of Abraham, the God of Isaac, the God of Jacob, the God of King David, the God of the prophets and the apostles is the God of our David's family even now. And He is still the God of our family, and all the families of the earth, even of those who are rejecting Him.

Our great God has chosen every one of us to transform us into the likeness of His beloved Son, Jesus Christ, and He adopts us into His great worldwide family, the Church. Whether individuals, or couples or parents with children, He laid down His life for us all. His agonizing, cruel death on the cross for us breaks our stony hearts over our disobedience toward Him. The glorious heavenly Father raised His Son from the dead. Now — as we repent from our sin — Jesus comes to live in us through His Holy Spirit to overflow His love and forgiveness through us to the unbelievers around us. Every biblically married couple, "one man with one woman united for life," every loving, faithfully united family and faithfully united Church, — united to obey God's written Word — is a testimony to the world that the heavenly Father sent His only begotten Son that we might live and love through Him.[112]

God, Creator of families, is building His own eternal family, training us for our future life in His own eternal, happy home. Jesus called that eternal, happy home *"My Father's house."* [113] Jesus called God: *"My Father and your Father, My God and your God."* [114] We, who belong to Jesus have reason to be joyful and hopeful even in the time of sorrow. We understand God's final purpose for our lives and for mankind. We are looking forward to the glorious final outcome.

Again, the example of Abraham, Isaac and Jacob stands before us. As they lived in the land that God had promised them they could have built cities, but they continued to live in tents because they knew that this present world is only our temporary home. Their heart was set on a better country, a heavenly country believing God's promise that He was building for them a heavenly city, the New Jerusalem. They testified that they were strangers in this present passing world and that they were preparing themselves to live forever in God's eternal home. It is because of this faith that the God of the Bible calls Himself *"the God of Abraham, the God of Isaac and the God of Jacob."* [115]

God showed the city of Abraham, Isaac and Jacob's longings to the apostle John in a vision:

> *"Then I, John, saw the holy city, New Jerusalem, coming down out of heaven from God, prepared as a bride adorned for her husband.*
> *And I heard a loud voice from heaven saying, 'Behold, the tabernacle of God is with men, and He will dwell with them and they shall be His people, God Himself will be with them and be their God.*
> *And God will wipe away every tear from their eyes, there shall be no more death, nor sorrow, nor crying. There shall be no more pain for the former things have passed away.'*
> *Then He who sat on the throne said: 'Behold, I make all things new . . . "* Revelation 21:2-6

> *"I will extol You, my God, O King . . .*
> *All your saints will tell of the glory of Your kingdom and speak of Your might,*
> *So that all men may know of Your mighty acts and the glorious splendor of Your kingdom."* Psalm 145:1, 11,12

Let us join our Lord Jesus Christ in His prayer that He prayed for us, the Father's family, at the Last Supper:

". . . Holy Father, keep through Your name those whom You have given Me, that they may be one even as We are one . . .

that they all may be one, as You Father, are in Me, and I in You, that they also may be one in Us, that the world may believe that You sent Me." John 17:11b, 21-23

"Even so, come, Lord Jesus!" Revelation 22:20b

Postscript

The Ten Commandments, "written with the finger of God," are our treasures enabling us to live in a peaceful, well functioning and lasting society. **Deuteronomy 9:10**

In the Ten Commandments God promises His mercy to the children of those fore-fathers who love Him and obey His commandments. **Deuteronomy 5:10**

America is still enjoying God's mercies because of the obedience of the founding fathers who established our laws on God's Word, the Bible, in order to invoke His favor on our nation.

The God of the Bible made America the greatest nation on earth because its citizens lived according to God's commandments and the disobedient were punished. **Deuteronomy 4:6-9**

God offers the same mercies to everyone all over the world, because of the obedience of His beloved Son, the Lord Jesus Christ, who was crucified in our place to pay the punishment for our disobedience to His commandments. God raised His Son from the dead. From His glory He gives His Holy Spirit to all those who receive His forgiveness and are willing to be made into loving, obedient children to the heavenly Father.

Sadly, at this time, in America godless citizens — in their blindness — are working to rob our nation of the knowledge of God and His Word, the treasure whereby God shed His grace on us. God cannot bless disobedient people!

We must lay hold of God's promise:

> *"If My people who are called by My name will humble themselves and pray and seek My face and turn from their wicked ways, then I will hear from heaven, and I will forgive their sin and heal their land.*
>
> *Now My eyes will be open and My ears attentive to prayer made in this place. For now I have chosen and sanctified this house,* **[God's household, God's family]***, that My name may be there forever; and My eyes and my heart will be there perpetually."* 2 Chronicles 7:14-16

About the Authors

Colonel Philip L. Steers, Jr. is a World War II veteran. Maria Vago Steers is his Hungarian-born war bride.

Philip Steers was born in Elmhurst, Long Island in 1917 and grew up during the Great Depression. He had to work while earning his college degree in accounting and his CPA. During World War II he served in North Africa and Europe. At the close of the war he was assigned to the U.S. Military Government in Munich Germany. He fell in love with a refugee from the Russians, Maria Vago, who worked in his office.

After Philip Steers returned to America he sent for her and married her in 1947 upon her arrival in Atlanta, GA. They lived in Vienna, Austria while he served with the U.S. Economic Aid Mission and in the Panama Canal Zone while he was the Financial Vice President of the Panama Canal Company for more than twenty years. The Panama Canal Zone was a delightful place for the raising of their four children, two boys, two girls.

In 1998 their second son David was ripped out of the family by tragic death. He was a loving father of his young family. His wife Leann was expecting their third child.

David left behind the inspiring testimony of his knowledge of the God of the Bible who sent His Son Jesus Christ to bless his family, whether in joy or in sorrow. David is still a challenge to his loved ones to get to know Him as the God of their whole family.[116]

Philip and Maria's calling before the Lord for their old age is from Psalm 78:1-8. They are to pass on the praises of the great God of the Bible to their fifteen grandchildren and their two great-grandchildren and to all the next generations, with the prayer that they, too, would dedicate themselves to love Him by obeying Him and by making Him known to the next generation from generation to generation.

Books by Mária Vágó Steers

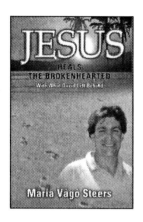

Jesus Heals the Broken Hearted
With What David Left Behind

ISBN 1-591606-84-5

2003 — English
Xulon Press
Xulon Press Books are available in bookstores every where and on the web at www.XulonPress.com

JÉZUS MEGGYÓGYÍT EGY SEBZETT SZÍVET
Bizonyságtétel az isteni kegyelmro˝l

ISBN 963 9390 18 6

2002 – Hungarian
Keresztyén Ismeretterjeszto˝ Alapítvány
1135 Budapest, Béke u. 35/A
Email: kia.kiadohivatal@mail.datanet.hu

Endnotes

[1] 1 John 2:24

[2] John 10:10

[3] 2 Corinthians 11;13, 14

[4] Deuteronomy 9:10

[5] Deuteronomy 5:10

[6] See Deuteronomy 4:6,7 together with 6-12

[7] Hebrews 2:13; 3:6; 5:8,9

[8] John 13:34, 35

[9] Psalm 65:1-5; 1 John 3:22, 5:14

[10] The book: "Jesus Heals The Brokenhearted" by Mária Vágó Steers, Xulon Press, tells David's full story. This book is also available in the Hungarian language, email <kia.kiadohivatal@mail.datanet.hu>

[11] Acts 2:36

[12] Acts 2::1 KJ

[13] Genesis 4:1

[14] Revelation 19:7, 8

[15] John 2:1-11

[16] John 20:31

[17] 1 Timothy 3:15

[18] Genesis 2:7

[19] Matthew 19:8

[20] Matthew 24:1-15; 2 Timothy 3:1-9

[21] Psalm 139; Romans 2:16

[22] see the concluding message of this book

[23] 2 Timothy 4:4 , Living Bible

[24] Isaiah 54:8-10

[25] James 2:23

[26] Genesis 17:19

[27] Genesis 21:1-3

[28] Romans 4:17

[29] Genesis 22:2 in The Douay Bible (1955) "…offer Isaac for a holocaust"

[30] Genesis 22:2; Hebrews 11:17

[31] Acts 3:25, 26

[32] Romans 4:11

[33] "righteous" means "pleasing to God"

[34] Romans 10:8-13

[35] Revelation 1:20

[36] Acts 2:32-36

[37] Genesis 17:16

[38] Hebrews 11:11

[39] Romans 10:17

[40] Genesis 17:7

[41] Exodus 2:1-10

[42] Exodus 2:23-26

[43] Exodus 3:15

[44] Luke 20:17

[45] Exodus 3:1-16

[46] Exodus 11:7

[47] Hebrews 11:16, with verses 13-16; Revelation 21:1-6

[48] 1 John 5:19; Revelation 11:8

[49] Galatians 1:4; 3:8; 1 Corinthians 11:31

[50] Deuteronomy 34:5; Joshua 1:1

[51] Exodus 14:4

[52] Exodus 15:1-21

[53] Exodus 16:12-21; 17:6

[54] see Postscript

[55] Exodus 29:42

[56] John 5:46

[57] Exodus 40:34; 13:21

[58] James 4:7-10

[59] 1 Corinthians 14:24, 25

[60] Deuteronomy 34:5-10

[61] Joshua 6:25

[62] Matthew 1:5

[63] 1 Timothy 3:15b

[64] Acts 13:22

[65] Isaiah 66:1

[66] Matthew 22:41-45

[67] Luke 2:11

[68] Isaiah 7:14; 9:6, 7

[69] 2 Samuel 7:25

[70] Luke 1:38

[71] 1 Corinthians 6:18-20

[72] Ephesians 2:10

[73] Revelation 7:9

[74] Revelation 7:9

[75] Luke 1:33

[76] Matthew 20:19

[77] Psalm 22; Isaiah chapter 53

[78] Genesis 15:4

[79] 2 Samuel 7:12

[80] Psalm 110:1,2; Matthew 22:41-46

[81] Psalm 78:32-41

[82] Jeremiah chapter 52

[83] Deuteronomy 4:24

[84] Deuteronomy 28:15-68

[85] Psalm 25:8

[86] Galatians 3:13-16

[87] 1 Corinthians 11:32

[88] John 12:31-33; Acts 2:32-36

[89] Acts 2:1-33

[90] Romans 1:1,2; 10:17

[91] Philippians 2:13

[92] Matthew 7:7

[93] Acts 3:25, 26

[94] Matthew 27:51

[95] Hebrews 10:19-25

[96] Matthew 6:9, 10; John 17:13, 21-23

[97] Acts 2:1 KJ

[98] Matthew 25:40; 18:5

[99] the Spanish word for "whole burnt offering"

[100] Psalm 65:1-5, 1 John 3:22, 5:14

[101] Revelation 5:8, 8:4; 2 Corinthians 2:14-17

[102] 2 Corinthians 1:11, 5:15

103

[104] Psalm 1:3; 1 Corinthians 15:57, 58
[105] 1 Thessalonians 2:19, 20
[106] Psalm 96:13; Revelation 1:7; 6:16, 17
[107] From Jefferson's notes on the State of Virginia, 1781
[108] Matthew 7:24-29; John 10:4; 12:48
[109] Romans 2:16
[110] Hebrews 3:12, 13
[111] 1 Peter 5:8
[112] Ezekiel 36:26; John 13:34,35; 1 John 3:16, 4:7-11
[113] John 2:16
[114] John 20:17
[115] Hebrews 11:13-16
[116] This family experience is found in the book "Jesus Heals The Brokenhearted" by Maria Vago Steers, published by Xulon Press.

Printed in the United States
21052LVS00007B/418-669

9 781594 677021